blended soups

blended soups

ELSA PETERSEN-SCHEPELERN

with photography by Jeremy Hopley

RYLAND
PETERS
& SMALL

Publishing Director	Anne Ryland
Head of Design	Gabriella Le Grazie
Designer	Ashley Western
Design Assistant	Sailesh Patel
Editorial Assistant	Maddalena Bastianelli
Production	Patricia Harrington
Food Stylists	Elsa Petersen-Schepelern, Fiona Smith
Stylist	Wei Tang
Photographer's Assistant	Karen Thomas
Author Photograph	Francis Loney

Acknowledgements

My thanks to my nephew Luc Votan for his expert advice, to my sister
Kirsten and to Fiona Smith for her guiding hand with food styling.

Notes

All spoon measurements are level unless otherwise noted.
Raw or partly cooked eggs should not be served to the very young, the old,
the frail, or to pregnant women.
Specialist Asian ingredients are available in large supermarkets, Thai,
Chinese, Japanese and Vietnamese shops, as well as Asian stores.

First published in Great Britain in 1999
by Ryland Peters & Small
Cavendish House, 51–55 Mortimer Street,
London W1N 7TD

Text © Elsa Petersen-Schepelern 1999
Design and photographs © Ryland Peters & Small 1999

Printed and bound in China by Toppan Printing Co.

ISBN 1 84172 008 9

A CIP record for this book is available from the British Library

contents

INTRODUCTION

What did we do
before the invention of
blenders, food processors,
spice grinders and their ilk?
A lot of hard work,
that's what!

These kitchen appliances are especially useful in making soups – turning vegetables into creamy purées, beans into a crunchy mixture, spices into powders or pastes, meat and poultry into delicious fillings for wontons and dumplings. The soups in this book are suitable for quick meals at home or for grander occasions such as dinner parties. I've even served them in mini-quantities at parties. They're so fast and easy, I don't know why people bother buying ready-made ones full of preservatives!

Home-made Stocks

You must have good stock, either home-made or bought from the supermarket. Being the world's laziest cook, I make mine in a microwave: it's quick, easy and clearer than the traditional kind. Put crushed parsley stalks, 1 onion, 1 carrot and 1 celery stalk, all chopped, in a lidded microwave dish. Add 500 g chicken pieces such as wings, or meat bones and trimmings, fill with boiling water and microwave on HIGH for 35 minutes. Let stand for 30 minutes, then strain off the liquid and discard the solids. Cool at room temperature until the fat rises to the surface, then chill. Remove and discard the fat, then use the stock within 1–2 days or freeze. (Strain at least 4 times through muslin for a clearer stock.) For vegetable stocks, omit the chicken, add extra vegetables and microwave on HIGH for 20 minutes, then let stand for 20 minutes.

VEGETABLES

Peel and core the peppers with a vegetable peeler and chop the flesh into the blender. Add the yellow tomatoes and crushed garlic and blend to a vibrant yellow purée. Add the stock and 250 ml crushed ice and blend again. Season well, then chill until very cold. Using a mandoline, slice the cucumber and radishes paper-thin.

Pour the purée into a glass soup tureen or separate bowls or glasses, adding extra ice if preferred. Top with the cucumbers, radishes, spring onions and red cherry tomatoes. Serve, sprinkled with the herbs, salt and cracked black pepper.

yellow gazpacho

4 yellow or orange peppers
1 punnet yellow cherry tomatoes, halved
2 garlic cloves, crushed with salt
750 ml chicken or vegetable stock
1 mini cucumber, halved lengthways
  and deseeded
6 radishes
4 spring onions, sliced
4 red cherry tomatoes, quartered
a few sprigs of parsley, chopped
a handful of chives, snipped (optional)
small sprigs of mint or basil
salt and cracked black pepper, to taste

serves 4–6

I'm not usually a fan of gazpacho, because the blended kind sometimes looks decidedly khaki. This one is a colourful exception, with clear, bright tastes. I think peppers are vastly improved when peeled, so use a vegetable peeler before coring.

coconut vichyssoise

I'm rather a fan of vichyssoise – and of coconut – and thought it was an inspired idea to put the two together. I prefer this soup hot or warm rather than cold, but please yourself.

Melt the butter and oil in a saucepan, add the onion and leeks and sauté gently until softened but not at all coloured.

Add the potatoes, stock and salt and simmer until the potatoes are soft, about 20 minutes. Transfer to a blender and purée until smooth. Add the coconut milk and enough extra stock to produce a thick, creamy consistency. Reheat if necessary, then serve hot or warm, with a trail of cream on top and your choice of other toppings, such as scissor-snipped chives or toasted fresh coconut.

1 tablespoon butter

1 tablespoon corn or sunflower oil

1 onion, finely sliced

3 leeks, white only, sliced

2 large potatoes, sliced

250 ml chicken or vegetable stock, plus extra (see method)

250 ml canned coconut milk

a pinch of sea salt

To serve, your choice of:

4 tablespoons single cream

scissor-snipped chives or Chinese chives

slivers of fresh coconut, lightly toasted

serves 4

carrot and ginger soup

with limes and clementines

Grated zest of limes and clementines give a certain spark to this golden gingery soup. I like the mild taste of clementine juice, but orange, mandarin or satsuma juice would also be good.

2 tablespoons butter or sunflower oil

2 tablespoons sunflower oil

2 onions, chopped

3 cm fresh ginger, finely chopped

500 g carrots (about 4–6), finely sliced

1 litre chicken stock or water

juice of 5 clementines (about 200 ml)

sea salt and freshly ground black pepper

shreds of lime and clementine zest, to serve

serves 4

Heat the butter and oil in a saucepan, add the onions and a pinch of salt and cook until softened and golden. Add the ginger and carrots and sauté a few minutes more. Add the stock or water, the clementine juice and seasoning. Bring to the boil, then simmer until the carrots are tender, about 20 minutes.

Strain into a jug, put the solids into a blender with 1–2 ladles of strained liquid, then purée, adding extra liquid if necessary. When smooth, add the remaining liquid and purée again.

Reheat if necessary, taste and adjust the seasoning, then serve the soup in bowls and top with lime and clementine zest.

fresh tomato soup with lemon and basil

My sister in Australia grows the world's most wonderful tomatoes. This recipe is based on her delicious bottled tomatoes, though unfortunately my store-bought fruit aren't a patch on hers!

1 kg very ripe red tomatoes
500 ml flavourful chicken stock
juice and shredded zest of 1 lemon
4 tablespoons pesto (optional)
a bunch of chives, scissor-snipped, or basil
sea salt and coarsely crushed black pepper

serves 4

To skin the tomatoes, cut a cross in the base of each, put in a bowl and cover with boiling water. Remove after 10 seconds and put into a strainer set over a large saucepan. Slip off and discard the skins and cut the tomatoes in half. Using a teaspoon, deseed into the strainer and put the tomatoes into the blender. Press the juice through the strainer and add to the blender, discarding the seeds.

Purée the tomatoes, adding a little of the stock to help the process. Add the remaining stock, season to taste and transfer to the saucepan. Heat well without boiling (to keep the fresh flavour).

Serve in heated soup plates with a spoonful of lemon juice, pesto if using, chives or basil, lemon zest and crushed black pepper.

beetroot soup with lemon zest

Put the chopped beetroot into a blender, add 2 ladles of stock and purée until smooth. Add the remaining stock and purée again. Test for thickness and seasoning, adding extra stock or water if the purée is too thick. Blend again.

Serve hot or chilled, topped with your choice of sour cream or crème fraîche, beetroot strips and grated lemon zest.

5 cooked beetroot, 4 coarsely chopped and 1 sliced into fine strips
750 ml chicken or vegetable stock
sea salt and freshly ground black pepper

To serve (optional):
4 tablespoons sour cream or crème fraîche
grated lemon zest

serves 4

chilled cucumber cream

Using a teaspoon, scrape the seeds out of the cucumbers and discard. Chop the flesh and skins coarsely, then transfer to a blender or food processor. Add the yoghurt, dried mint, garlic and 125 ml crushed ice and blend to a green-flecked purée.

Taste and adjust the seasoning, then serve in chilled soup plates, topped with sprigs of mint.

4 mini cucumbers or 1 large cucumber (about 500 g), halved lengthways
1 kg plain yoghurt
3 tablespoons dried mint
1 fat garlic clove, crushed
sea salt and coarsely crushed black pepper
sprigs of mint, to serve

serves 4

The blended element of this soup is *pistou*, the Provençal version of pesto. You need a big bunch of scented summertime basil.

1 tablespoon olive oil
1 red onion, cut into wedges
1 potato, diced
a handful of soup pasta, such as ditalini
1 litre clear chicken or vegetable stock*
250 g cooked or canned cannellini beans
salt and freshly ground black pepper

Your choice of:
4 baby carrots, halved lengthways
4 Brussels sprouts, halved
4 baby courgettes, halved lengthways
1 red pepper, peeled, cored and sliced
a handful of green peas
a handful of shelled broad beans
2 flat beans, cut into short lengths

Pistou:
leaves from 1 large bunch basil
2 garlic cloves, crushed
4 tablespoons grated Parmesan cheese
olive oil (see method)

serves 4

soupe au pistou

To make the pistou, put the basil, garlic and Parmesan in a blender or food processor and blend as finely as possible. Add enough olive oil in a steady stream to form a loose paste. Set aside.

Heat the oil in a small frying pan, add the onion and fry on both sides until softened. Cook the potato and soup pasta in boiling salted water until tender. Drain. Blanch your choice of carrots, sprouts, courgettes, pepper, peas, broad beans or flat beans in boiling salted water until tender but crisp, about 3–5 minutes. Drain and refresh in cold water. Pop the broad beans out of their grey skins and discard the skins.

Bring the stock to the boil and add the seasoning, pasta and all vegetables including the cannellini beans. Simmer for 2 minutes or until heated through. Serve in heated soup plates, with a separate bowl of pistou. Guests stir the pistou into their soup to taste.

Note: For a clear stock, strain it at least 4 times through muslin.

1 onion, finely chopped

2 garlic cloves, crushed

3 cm fresh ginger, finely chopped

2 stalks lemongrass, finely chopped

2 red chillies, sliced, plus extra to serve

3 limes, 1 juiced, 2 cut into wedges

3 tablespoons peanut oil

500 g sweet potatoes (about 2 large), cut into large chunks

about 500 ml canned coconut milk

500 ml chicken stock

sea salt and freshly ground black pepper

serves 4

sweet potato soup

To make the spice paste, put the onion, garlic, ginger, lemongrass, chillies, lime juice and half the oil in a blender or spice grinder and purée until smooth (add a little water if necessary).

Heat the remaining oil in a saucepan. Add the spice paste and stir-fry gently for 5 minutes. Add the sweet potatoes, coconut milk and stock. Simmer until the sweet potatoes are soft.

Transfer to a blender, purée until smooth, season to taste, reheat if necessary, top with sliced chillies and serve with wedges of lime.

roasted red pepper soup with rocket

Heat the oil in a frying pan, add the onions and sauté gently until soft and golden. Push to the side of the pan, add the garlic and sauté for about 1 minute.

Meanwhile, halve and deseed the peppers, put on a sheet of foil or a baking sheet under a hot grill and cook until the skin is black and charred. Transfer to a bowl or saucepan and cover tightly with clingfilm or a lid. Leave for about 10 minutes to steam, then transfer to a strainer set over the same bowl or pan. Scrape off and discard the skins (keep a few of the nice brown toasty bits if you like), putting the flesh back into the bowl or pan (catch as many of the toasted juices as possible).

Transfer to a blender, add the onions and garlic and work to a purée, adding a little stock if necessary. Add the remaining stock and purée again, then transfer to a saucepan and heat to boiling point. Remove from the heat, season, then serve in heated soup plates.

Top with wild rocket, fresh thyme leaves or small sprigs of oregano. For extra toasted flavour, add a few shards of toasted pepper skin to each bowl of soup.

Note: For relentless hotheads, a couple of medium-hot red chillies such as fresno or serrano may be char-grilled at the same time as the peppers and treated in the same way.

2 tablespoons olive oil
2 onions, halved and finely sliced
2 garlic cloves, crushed
8 long red peppers (or yellow or orange)
1 litre chicken or vegetable stock
sea salt and freshly ground black pepper
a bunch of wild rocket, thyme or oregano

serves 4

japanese fresh corn soup

with spring onions and tamari soy sauce

Bring a large saucepan of water to the boil, add the corn and simmer for about 15 minutes. Drain. Hold the cobs upright on a chopping board, blunt end down. Run a sharp knife down the cobs, shaving off the kernels.

Put the kernels into a blender with 250 ml stock. Purée until smooth, then press through a strainer into a saucepan. Return the corn to the blender, add another ladle of stock, purée, then strain as before, pushing through as much corn juice as possible. Repeat until all the stock is used. Reheat the mixture.

Put 1 egg yolk, if using, into each of 4 small soup bowls, ladle the soup on top and beat with chopsticks (the hot soup cooks the egg). Serve, topped with spring onions, tamari or soy sauce and pepper to taste.

Note: Dashi stock is sold in powder or concentrate form in many supermarkets and Asian stores. However, it's easy and nicer to make your own (the ingredients are sold in the same shops). Put a sheet of kombu seaweed about 5 x 5 cm in a saucepan with 1 litre cold water. Bring it slowly to the boil over a gentle heat. Just before boiling, remove the kombu. Stir in 25 g grated dried bonito, turn off the heat and let cool. When the bonito has settled to the bottom, skim off any foam, then strain the stock and use. The kombu and bonito can be used to make a second batch. The stock will keep in the fridge for 3 days, or can be frozen. (Kombu is often toasted first, by waving it briefly over a gas flame, or heating very briefly for about 30 seconds under a hot grill.)

4 fresh corn cobs or about 500 g fresh corn kernels

1 litre hot dashi stock* or chicken stock

To serve, your choice of:
4 egg yolks (optional)
4 spring onions, sliced diagonally
2 tablespoons tamari or dark soy sauce
cracked black pepper, or a Japanese pepper mixture
**   such as furikake seasoning or seven-spice**

serves 4

A variation on a traditional Japanese summer soup, prized for the
fresh taste of corn – and very easy to make.

A few dried porcini mushrooms will give a stronger mushroom flavour to a soup made with ordinary cultivated mushrooms. Use large, open field mushrooms to give a deeper colour.

Put the dried porcini in a bowl, add 250 ml boiling water and let soak for about 15 minutes. Heat the oil in a frying pan, add the fresh mushrooms and sauté until coloured but still firm.

Add the onion to the frying pan and sauté until softened, then add the garlic, nutmeg and parsley. Rinse any grit out of the porcini and strain their soaking liquid several times through muslin. Add the liquid and the porcini to the pan (reserve a few small ones for garnish). Bring to the boil, then transfer to a blender. Reserve a few of the sautéed mushroom for garnish and add the remaining mushroom mixture to the blender. Add 2 ladles of the boiling chicken stock, then blend to a purée.

Heat the butter in a saucepan, stir in the flour and cook gently, stirring continuously, until the mixture is very dark brown (take care or it will burn). Add the remaining stock, 1 ladle at a time, stirring well after each addition. Add the mushroom mixture, bring to the boil, then simmer for 20 minutes. Add salt and pepper to taste, then serve topped with a few reserved mushrooms, coarsely chopped parsley and a dollop of crème fraîche.

25 g dried porcini mushrooms
4 tablespoons olive oil
6 large, open-capped field mushrooms, wiped, trimmed and sliced
1 onion, halved and finely sliced
3 garlic cloves, crushed
a pinch of freshly grated nutmeg
leaves from a large bunch of parsley, finely chopped in a food processor
1.25 litres boiling chicken stock
4 tablespoons butter
4 tablespoons flour
sea salt and freshly ground black pepper

To serve:
4–6 tablespoons coarsely chopped parsley
4–6 tablespoons crème fraîche

serves 4–6

italian mushroom soup

with porcini and parsley

cream of broccoli soup

with leeks and broad beans

A pale green, fresh, summery soup that can be adapted to other ingredients – it's also good with cauliflower and cannellini beans.

Heat the butter and oil in a large saucepan, add the leeks and fry gently until softened but not browned. Reserve a few spoonfuls of the cooked leeks for garnish.

Add the broccoli to the pan and stir-fry until green. Add the potato, stock and 1 litre water and bring to the boil. Reduce the heat, add salt and pepper and simmer for 30 minutes.

Pop the cooked broad beans out of their grey skins and discard the skins. Reserve a few spoonfuls of broad beans for garnish.

Strain the soup into a bowl and put the solids and the broad beans in a blender. Add 2 ladles of the strained liquid and purée until smooth. Add the remaining liquid and blend again. Reheat the soup, pour into heated soup bowls, top with the reserved leeks and skinned broad beans, then serve.

2 tablespoons butter

2 tablespoons corn or sunflower oil

2 large leeks, chopped

1 head broccoli, broken into florets

1 potato, chopped

600 ml vegetable or chicken stock

200 g shelled, cooked broad beans

sea salt and freshly ground black pepper

serves 4

A favourite soup in the Antipodes, usually made with boiled pumpkin, but I rather like the smoky taste of this baked variety. A sprinkle of freshly ground nutmeg can be added at the end.

1 kg pumpkin, cut into wedges
sunflower or corn oil, for roasting and frying
1 litre chicken stock
2 large potatoes, cut into chunks
250 ml milk
4 tablespoons sour cream
salt and freshly ground black pepper

serves 4

pumpkin soup

To make pumpkin crisps, cut about 20 fine slices off one of the wedges of pumpkin with a vegetable peeler, so you get an edge of green skin. Set aside.

Peel and deseed the remaining pumpkin and cut into large chunks. Brush a baking sheet with oil, add the pumpkin chunks and brush them with oil too. Put in a preheated oven at 200°C (400°F) Gas 6 and cook until browned outside and soft and fluffy inside, about 30 minutes, according to the size of the chunks.

Meanwhile, bring the chicken stock to the boil, add the potatoes and cook for about 20 minutes until soft. Put the potatoes into a blender and reserve the stock.

Pour about 3 cm depth of oil into a wok and heat until a piece of bread will brown in 30 seconds. Add the fine slices of pumpkin and deep-fry until crispy. Remove and drain on crumpled kitchen paper.

Add the roasted pumpkin to the blender, add seasoning, milk and a ladle of hot stock. Purée until smooth and creamy, adding more stock if necessary. (You may have to work in batches, according to the size of your blender.)

Transfer to a clean saucepan, season to taste and reheat to just below boiling point. Ladle into heated soup bowls, top with a swirl of sour cream and a few pumpkin crisps and serve with crusty bread.

1 fresh corn cob

2 tablespoons sunflower or corn oil

½ onion, diced

1 yellow pepper, peeled and sliced

1 red pepper, peeled and sliced

2 red tomatoes, peeled and deseeded

1 tablespoon fresh thyme leaves

1 tablespoon fresh oregano leaves

sea salt and freshly ground black pepper

1 punnet yellow cherry tomatoes, halved,

to serve (optional)

serves 4

mexican salsa soup

Put the corn, blunt end down, on a board and shave off the kernels with a sharp knife. Put the oil and kernels in a saucepan and stir-fry gently for about 5 minutes. Remove from the heat.

Put all the remaining ingredients (except the yellow tomatoes) in a food processor and pulse briefly until chopped but still chunky.

Add to the pan, then cook gently for 6–8 minutes. Serve topped with halved yellow cherry tomatoes, if using.

Everyone likes a spicy Mexican salsa. This is my favourite, turned into a soup – make it in a food processor for a coarser texture. Cut the peppers in half and peel with a vegetable peeler.

This very simple soup is packed with taste, thanks to the blended flavourings. Don't worry if you don't have all of them – onion, garlic and ginger are the most important. If you don't have tamarind paste, stir in a squeeze of lime juice instead.

To make the spice paste, put the lemongrass, lime leaves or zest, onion, garlic and ginger in a blender and purée until smooth.

Put the stock in a saucepan, add the tomatoes and spice paste and bring to the boil. Simmer for 5–10 minutes. Add the fish and fish sauce or soy. Poach for 5 minutes until opaque (do not let boil).

Put the pieces of fish and tomatoes in large soup bowls, stir the tamarind paste into the stock, return to the boil, then ladle over the fish. Serve topped with sprigs of coriander.

asian fish soup

with ginger and tomatoes

1.5 litres fish stock

6 tomatoes, skinned and deseeded

1 kg thick white fish fillets, such as cod or haddock, cut in thick slices

1 tablespoon fish sauce or soy sauce

1 tablespoon smooth tamarind paste (see opposite)

sprigs of coriander, to serve

Spice paste:

1 stalk lemongrass, finely sliced

2 kaffir lime leaves, very finely sliced, or a curl of lime zest

1 onion, finely sliced

3 garlic cloves, crushed

3 cm fresh ginger, finely chopped

serves 4

provençal fish soup with rouille

Clean all the fish and seafood and cut the large pieces of fish into chunks. Put the mussels or clams, if using, in a large saucepan with 1 tablespoon water, cover and heat until they open, shaking the pan from time to time. Remove and set aside as they open.

Heat the oil in a large frying pan, add the onion and leek, if using, and cook until softened and translucent. Add the tomatoes, garlic, bay leaves, saffron and seasoning. Simmer for 10 minutes. Add the fish, seafood and water or stock, bring to the boil, reduce the heat and simmer until the fish is opaque, about 2–3 minutes.

To make the rouille, put the bread in a bowl, sprinkle with about 1 tablespoon water, squeeze together, then squeeze dry. Put the egg yolk, garlic, chillies and bread in a blender and purée until smooth. With the motor running, gradually add enough olive oil to make a thick paste. (If you're concerned about raw egg, omit it.)

Divide the fish and seafood between large bowls, then ladle in the liquid. Serve the toast, rouille and grated cheese separately.

To eat, spread the slices of toasted baguette with rouille, add to the soup and sprinkle with grated cheese.

1 kg assorted fish fillets and seafood
12–20 mussels and/or clams (optional)
125 ml extra-virgin olive oil
1 onion, sliced
1 large leek, sliced (optional)
3 large tomatoes, skinned and chopped
3 large garlic cloves, crushed
3 small fresh bay leaves
1 sachet saffron powder
1 litre water or fish stock
sea salt and freshly ground black pepper

Rouille:
2 thick slices fresh French-style bread
1 egg yolk (see method)
3 garlic cloves, crushed
2 dried red chillies, deseeded and crushed
olive oil (see method)

To serve:
1 small bowl grated cheese, such as Gruyère
1 baguette, sliced diagonally and toasted

serves 4

Rouille, the peppery Provençal sauce, is the blended element of this soup. Delicious with many dishes, it is traditional with fish soup.

A bisque is a soup made with shellfish like prawns, crabs or lobster – a blender or food processor is the easiest way to make it. If fresh prawns are too expensive, Chinese dried shrimp have great flavour.

Put the dried shrimp and saffron threads, if using, in a small bowl and cover with boiling water. Set aside until the shrimp soften.

Heat the oil in a large, heavy-based saucepan, add the shallots and sauté until softened and translucent. Add the garlic and prawn shells and stir-fry until aromatic. Add the stock, bay leaf, dried shrimp and saffron and their soaking liquid. Boil hard for about 5 minutes so the stock and oil amalgamate. Add the harissa, fish and prawns and poach for 5 minutes until the fish is opaque.

Remove the bay leaf, strain the soup into a bowl or jug and transfer the solids, including the shells, to a blender. Add 1–2 ladles of stock and blend until smooth. Push the mixture through a strainer into the rinsed saucepan, then transfer the solids back into the blender. Add more stock, blend again and push through a strainer again. Repeat until all the stock has been used. The more you blend and push, the stronger the flavour will be.

Discard the solids in the strainer and reheat the soup in the saucepan. Stir in the lemon juice and salt to taste, then serve. The toast and rouille (page 36) would also be delicious with this soup.

1 packet Chinese dried shrimp (about 50 g)
a large pinch of saffron threads or 1 sachet saffron powder
2 tablespoons olive oil
2 large shallots, chopped
2 garlic cloves, crushed
1 kg whole prawns, cooked or uncooked, shells reserved, or 1 extra pack dried shrimp
1 litre fish stock
1 bay leaf
2 tablespoons harissa paste
1 kg fish fillets, such as snapper or redfish
juice of ½ lemon
sea salt

serves 4

prawn bisque

This soup is usually made with peeled artichokes, but I find that they discolour quickly and are hard to peel. This method is very easy – choose large artichokes with as few knobbles as possible.

Boil the artichokes until tender. Drain, cool a little, then press the flesh out of the skins. Discard the skins and cooking water. Put the stock in a large saucepan, add the fish, bring to the boil, then turn off the heat and leave for 5 minutes. Transfer the fish to a plate, remove and discard the skin and bones, break the flesh into large pieces, cover and keep it warm. Reserve the stock in the pan.

Heat the oil in a frying pan, add the bacon and cook until crisp. Remove the bacon and drain on kitchen paper. Add the butter to the pan, add the leek and sauté until translucent (do not let brown). Add the garlic and sauté for 1 minute. Transfer to the saucepan, add the artichokes, potatoes, herbs, seasoning and water to cover. Simmer for 20 minutes. Remove the herbs, add the milk, transfer to a blender and purée until smooth, adding extra boiling water if the mixture is too thick. Put the fish in heated soup bowls, ladle in the chowder, and serve topped with bacon and thyme or bay leaf.

500 g Jerusalem artichokes, unpeeled

300 ml fish or chicken stock

about 500 g smoked fish, such as haddock

1 tablespoon olive oil

2 slices smoked bacon, cut crossways
    into 3 cm pieces

1 tablespoon butter

1 leek, white only, finely sliced

1 garlic clove, crushed

2 potatoes, finely sliced

1 bay leaf

2 sprigs of thyme

300 ml hot milk

sea salt and freshly ground black pepper

serves 4

jerusalem artichoke chowder

with smoked haddock and crispy bacon

The blended element of this soup is the red curry paste. Make in quantity, then freeze in ice cube trays. Asian soups are quick and easy to make if you have the spice pastes ready to hand.

To make the curry paste, remove the seeds from the chillies if preferred. Stir-fry the coriander and cumin seeds in a dry frying pan for 2 minutes to release the aromas. Let cool. Put all the paste ingredients in a spice grinder or blender and purée in bursts. Use 2–4 tablespoons for this recipe and freeze the remainder.

Soak the rice stick noodles, if using, in hot water for 15 minutes. Boil for 1–2 minutes, then drain and plunge into cold water.

Put the stock in a saucepan, add the curry paste and bring to the boil. Add the aubergines, if using, and the beans. Return to the boil, simmer for 15 minutes, then stir in the fish sauce and sugar. Drain the noodles, cover with boiling water, then drain again.

Divide noodles and vegetables between large bowls. Add the beef, ladle in boiling stock (which instantly cooks the beef), and serve.

thai spicy beef soup

150 g dried wide rice stick noodles (optional)

500 ml chicken or beef stock

3 egg-shaped white or yellow aubergines, quartered and deseeded (optional)

6 snake beans, sliced into 3 cm pieces

2 tablespoons fish sauce

1 teaspoon sugar

125 g beef fillet, frozen, then finely sliced

Red Thai curry paste:

5–10 dried red chillies, soaked in hot water for 30 minutes, then drained

½ teaspoon coriander seeds

½ teaspoon cumin seeds

separated cloves from 1 whole garlic bulb

2–3 pink Thai shallots or 1 regular

3 cm fresh ginger or galangal, finely sliced

grated zest of 1 lime, preferably a kaffir lime

1 teaspoon sea salt

1 tablespoon fish sauce

serves 4

Delicious wonton fillings take seconds to make in a food processor.

wonton chicken soup

8 Chinese cabbage leaves

1 poached chicken breast, shredded

1 carrot, finely sliced lengthways, blanched

2 spring onions, finely sliced lengthways

a handful of fresh beansprouts, trimmed

Wontons:

125 g pork fillet or chicken breast, sliced

3 spring onions, chopped

a pinch of salt

1 teaspoon grated fresh ginger

2 water chestnuts, chopped

12 small wonton skins

1 egg white, lightly beaten with a fork

Chinese chicken stock:

1.5 litres chicken stock

4 whole star anise

5 cm fresh ginger, peeled and finely sliced

1 onion, sliced

salt, to taste

serves 4

Bring a large saucepan of water to the boil. Add the Chinese cabbage leaves and blanch for 1 minute. Plunge into a bowl of iced water for 5 minutes. Drain. Cut out and discard the white ribs. Put 4 leaves, one on top of the other, on a tea towel. Roll them up into a cylinder and press out the liquid. Cut the cylinder crossways into 3 cm long sections. Repeat with the other 4 leaves.

To make the wontons, put the pork or chicken in a food processor and pulse until minced. Add the spring onions, salt and ginger and pulse again. Transfer to a bowl and stir in the water chestnuts. Brush a circle of egg white around the centre of each wonton skin and put 1 teaspoon of mixture in the middle. Twirl the wonton skin around the filling to make a shuttlecock shape. Press to seal.

Put the stock ingredients in a saucepan and simmer for 10 minutes. Cool, strain, then strain through muslin at least 4 times to clarify the stock. Reheat, then poach the wontons for 1½ minutes. Divide the wontons, stock, chicken, cabbage and carrot between heated soup plates and top with the spring onions and beansprouts.

coconut laksa

with chicken and noodles

3 tablespoons peanut oil

500 ml canned coconut milk

2 boneless chicken breasts, skinned and thickly sliced

fish sauce or salt, to taste

750 g fresh or 100 g dried udon noodles

Spice paste:

3–6 red or orange chillies, cored and chopped

1 shallot, chopped

2 stalks lemongrass, finely sliced

3 cm fresh ginger, finely sliced

½ teaspoon ground turmeric

6 blanched almonds, chopped

1 tablespoon fish sauce or a pinch of salt

1 garlic clove, crushed

To serve:

1 packet fresh beansprouts, trimmed

4 spring onions, sliced diagonally

1 red chilli, cored and finely sliced

sprigs of fresh coriander (optional)

serves 4

Spice pastes are usually laboriously made with a mortar and pestle – a blender is an easy, modern alternative.

Put all the spice paste ingredients into a spice grinder or blender and work to a paste (add a little water if necessary).

Heat the oil in a wok, add the spice paste and cook gently for about 5 minutes. Add 1 litre boiling water, then the coconut milk, bring to the boil, stirring, then add the chicken and return to the boil. Reduce to a simmer and poach the chicken for 10–15 minutes or until cooked through. Add fish sauce or salt, to taste.

If using fresh noodles, rinse in cold water, then boil for about 1–2 minutes. If using dried noodles, cook in boiling unsalted water for 10–12 minutes, then drain. Divide the noodles between large soup bowls. Add the chicken and liquid, top with the beansprouts, spring onions, chilli and coriander, if using, and serve.

tomato and bean soup

with spicy harissa paste

A very quick and comforting soup on a cold winter night – a food processor will give a coarser, more interesting texture than a blender.

Put the tomatoes, beans and stock in a food processor, in batches if necessary, and pulse briefly until coarsely chopped but not smooth. Transfer to a saucepan, add the crushed garlic, lemon juice and harissa paste and heat to just below boiling, stirring. Thin with boiling water, if necessary. Season, then serve.

Variation: serve sprinkled with chopped parsley, scissor-snipped chives, grated Parmesan cheese and crusty bread on the side.

500 ml crushed Italian tomatoes

500 g cooked red kidney beans

500 ml chicken stock

2 garlic cloves, crushed

juice of 1 large lemon

2 tablespoons harissa paste or chilli paste

salt

serves 4–6

Many supermarkets sell ready-shelled peas, so this recipe can be made easily. If you cook the peas in a microwave, in the package, with little or no liquid, their flavour will be concentrated.

To cook the peas, microwave on HIGH for 3–4 minutes, or follow the package instructions. Alternatively, simmer in boiling water with a pinch of salt for about 2–3 minutes or until tender.

Meanwhile, heat the olive oil in a frying pan, add the pancetta and sauté until crispy. Remove and drain on crumpled kitchen paper.

Put the peas in a blender with 1–2 ladles of boiling stock. Work to a purée, adding extra stock if necessary. Add the remaining stock and blend again. Taste and adjust the seasoning. Reheat, thinning with a little boiling water if necessary, then ladle into heated soup bowls and serve, topped with crispy bacon and sprigs of mint.

550 g shelled peas (about 3 packs)

1 litre boiling chicken stock

sea salt and freshly ground black pepper

To serve:

1 tablespoon olive oil

8 slices pancetta or bacon, quartered

sprigs of mint

serves 4

fresh pea soup

with mint and crispy bacon

lebanese chickpea soup

with crème fraîche, pepper and parsley

1 litre boiling chicken stock

500 ml hoummus, ready-made or
   home-made (see below)

Home-made hoummus (optional):

425 g cooked or canned chickpeas
   (about 500 ml), drained if canned

2 tablespoons olive oil

1 onion, grated

3 garlic cloves, crushed

sea salt and freshly ground black pepper

chicken or vegetable stock (see method)

To serve:

4 tablespoons cream or crème fraîche

cracked black pepper

a handful of parsley leaves (optional)

serves 4

This soup version of hoummus is creamy and delicious. I include a recipe for home-made hoummus, but you can also use the store-bought variety if you're in a hurry.

If making your own hoummus, put all the ingredients except the stock in a blender and work to a smooth purée. Thin with stock to form a thick, spreadable consistency. Use 500 ml of the hoummus for the soup and reserve the rest for another use.

Put the hoummus in a blender, add 1 ladle of the boiling chicken stock and purée. Add the remaining stock and blend again. Reheat if necessary, then serve, topped with a trail of cream or crème fraîche, cracked pepper and a few parsley leaves, if using.

jamaican bean soup with chillies

200 g dried red beans, such as rose coco,
   rose cowpeas or red kidney beans
2 large onions, 1 quartered, 1 sliced in
   wedges to make petals, then separated
3 large garlic cloves, crushed
3 tablespoons olive oil
6 slices smoked bacon, coarsely chopped
1 baking potato, chopped
1 habanero chilli, pricked several times with
   a toothpick
1 large sprig of thyme
750 ml chicken stock or water
sea salt and freshly ground black pepper

To serve (optional):
crispy bacon
thyme leaves

serves 4

Put the beans in a measuring jug and make up to 750 ml with boiling water. Soak for a few hours or overnight. Drain and rinse.

Put in a saucepan with water to cover, bring to the boil, then boil hard for 10 minutes. Drain, return to the pan, add 750 ml cold water, the quartered onion and 1 crushed garlic clove. Bring to the boil and simmer for about 30 minutes or until tender. Drain.

Heat the oil in a stockpot or saucepan, add the bacon and sliced onion and cook until softened and translucent. Add the potato and the remaining garlic and cook until golden. Add the chilli, thyme, beans and stock, with salt and pepper to taste. Bring to the boil, simmer gently for about 15–30 minutes, then remove the thyme and chilli. If serving the chilli, deseed it and finely slice the flesh.

Put the beans, vegetables and cooking liquid in a blender and purée until smooth, in batches if necessary. Divide between heated soup plates. Serve, topped with crispy bacon, thyme leaves or the finely sliced chilli, if using.

In Jamaica, when a girl marries, her stockpot is the first thing she needs to set up house. It is the perfect pot for this soup, but if you don't have one, an ordinary heavy-based saucepan will have to do.

creamy french almond soup

This sumptuous soup is loosely based on the classic French Onion Soup. The broth is thickened with almond milk – a delicious alternative to cream, and perfect for people who 'don't do dairy'.

2 tablespoons olive oil

2 large onions, sliced

2 garlic cloves, crushed

125 ml white wine (optional)

1 litre boiling chicken or vegetable stock

200 g shelled almonds

1 baguette, finely sliced, then oven-toasted
   until golden

125 g Gruyère cheese or cheddar, grated
   into long strips

sea salt and freshly ground black pepper

serves 4

Heat the oil in a large, heavy-based saucepan, add the onion and sauté until softened and golden. Add the garlic and sauté for about 1 minute until golden. Add the wine, if using, and boil hard until reduced to 2 tablespoons. Add the stock and boil for 2 minutes.

Put the almonds in a blender or food processor and grind to a fine meal. Add half the wine-stock mixture and blend well. Pass through a fine strainer back into the saucepan, pressing through as much almond milk as possible. Return the nuts to the blender, add another 2–3 ladles of the liquid from the pan. Repeat, blending and straining, at least twice more, to extract as much almond milk as possible from the nuts. Add the almond milk to the remaining wine-stock mixture and season to taste.

Divide the soup between ovenproof bowls, top with a few slices of toast and some cheese and put under a hot grill for 1–2 minutes until the cheese begins to melt. Serve with extra grated cheese.

indian yellow lentil soup

with mustard seed tempering

South Indians must have the most wonderful vegetarian food ever invented. They have been vegetarian for thousands of years and the many kinds of lentils, known as *dhaal*, provide protein in the diet.

Put the channa dhaal, turmeric, cumin and chilli in a saucepan, cover with 1 litre cold water and bring to the boil. Simmer, covered, until tender (the time will depend on the age and variety). Purée in a blender, in batches if necessary. Transfer to a clean saucepan and stir in enough boiling stock to make a thick, soupy consistency. Reheat to just below boiling point, then taste and adjust the seasoning.

To make the tempering, heat the oil in a frying pan, add the mustard and cardamom seeds and fry until they pop. Add the onion and cook until lightly browned. Add the garlic and chilli, if using, and stir-fry for about 1 minute to release the aromas.

Serve the soup in bowls or cups, topped with a spoonful of tempering and a dollop of plain yoghurt, if using.

250 g channa dhaal or yellow split peas
½ teaspoon ground turmeric
½ teaspoon cumin seeds
1 small red dried chilli, deseeded
boiling vegetable stock (see method)
plain yoghurt, to serve (optional)
salt

Mustard seed tempering:
3 tablespoons corn or mustard oil or ghee
1 tablespoon mustard seeds
1 tablespoon cardamom seeds
1 onion, halved and finely sliced lengthways
2 fat garlic cloves, crushed
1 red chilli, cored and finely sliced (optional)

serves 4

My Danish ancestors were great fans of fruit soups as a first course or as a pudding. I grew up in tropical Australia, and if any mangoes survived the greedy attentions of children and cattle, we would have loved to make soup out of them. Alas, they never did!

Put the mango pulp in the blender with the ice, champagne, if using, the ginger purée, sliced stem ginger and the ginger syrup and blend until smooth. Add enough iced water to produce the consistency of thin cream. Serve in chilled soup bowls or glasses, and top with shreds of grated lime zest.

Notes: To purée fresh (ripe) mangoes, put the flesh in a blender with the juice of 1 lime or lemon. Blend until smooth. About 4 large mangoes produce 500 ml. To make ginger purée, break fresh ginger into pieces and soak in water for 1 hour. Drain, peel and slice, then blend with a little lemon juice or water until smooth. Freeze in ice cube trays and use when needed.

500 ml mango pulp, canned or fresh*

250 ml crushed ice

250 ml demi-sec champagne or more ice

2 tablespoons ginger purée*

4 pieces preserved stem ginger, finely sliced

4 tablespoons of syrup from the jar

grated zest of 2 limes

serves 4

chilled mango soup with champagne and ginger

watermelon soup with chilli flakes

Sweet watermelon tastes amazing blended
with the spicy prickle of dried chilli flakes.
Use the reddest, ripest melons you can find.

1 round, chilled, ripe watermelon, cut into wedges
1 tablespoon chilli flakes, plus extra, to serve
ice cubes, to serve (optional)

serves 4

Cut the seedless parts out of the watermelon and put
into the blender (reserve any juice).

Cut the seedy part out of each wedge and put it in a
sieve set over a bowl. Press the flesh through the sieve
(don't worry too much about getting it all), then
transfer the contents of the bowl to the blender.

Blend, in batches if necessary, until smooth. Add the
chilli, blend briefly, then serve in chilled soup plates
and add ice cubes, if using, and extra chilli flakes.

rockmelon soup with japanese pink pickled ginger

Use very scented melons, such as green Galia or orange Charentais. Don't chill the melons, or you will deaden their flavour.

2 ripe cantaloupe- or honeydew-style melons
500 ml crushed ice
1 tablespoon ground ginger
1 tablespoon freshly cracked black pepper
2 tablespoons chopped Japanese pink pickled ginger
sprigs of mint or borage flowers (optional)
ice cubes, to serve

serves 4

Halve and deseed the melons. Using a spoon, scoop out the flesh into a blender or food processor. Add the ice and ground ginger and work, in bursts, to a purée. Add enough iced water to make a pourable consistency.

Serve in bowls with ice cubes, pepper, pink pickled ginger and mint leaves or borage flowers, if using.